Arthur Rowley William Lascelles

A Treatise on the Nature and Cultivation of Coffee

With Some Remarks on the Management and Purchase of Coffee Estates

Arthur Rowley William Lascelles

A Treatise on the Nature and Cultivation of Coffee
With Some Remarks on the Management and Purchase of Coffee Estates

ISBN/EAN: 9783337025397

Printed in Europe, USA, Canada, Australia, Japan

Cover: Foto ©Andreas Hilbeck / pixelio.de

More available books at **www.hansebooks.com**

A TREATISE

ON

THE NATURE AND CULTIVATION

OF

COFFEE;

WITH SOME

REMARKS ON THE MANAGEMENT AND PURCHASE

OF

COFFEE ESTATES.

BY

ARTHUR R. W. LASCELLES,

MANAGING DIRECTOR, MOYAR COFFEE COMPANY (LIMITED).

LONDON:

SAMPSON LOW, SON, AND MARSTON,

MILTON HOUSE, LUDGATE HILL.

1865.

PREFACE.

In the following pages no pretensions are made to literary composition or elegance of diction. They are put forth simply as hints, both to those who purpose engaging actively in the cultivation of coffee, and as a guide to others who wish to know somewhat of the nature of the undertaking they are engaged in, when they subscribe for shares in any of the numerous coffee companies which are so frequently launched. During his planting experience of nearly a quarter of a century, the author has frequently, both in his own case and in that of others, had occasion to regret the absence of any such information as is here sought to be afforded, and if this publication should in any measure supply a need which is generally admitted, by those most acquainted with the subject, to be seriously felt by beginners, or should it lead to the subject being taken up by others more capable of dealing with it, the author's object will be obtained.

A. L.

61, MARK LANE, E.C.

CONTENTS.

———◆———

CHAPTER IX.

CHAPTER X.

CHAPTER XI.

CHAPTER XII.

CHAPTER XIII.—NOTE.

CHAPTER XIV.

APPENDIX.

ERRATA.

Page 3, line 7 from the top, for "Euarea" read "Enarea."

" 17, " 23 " "roomrie" read "koomrie."

" 22, " 18 " after "last" insert "lines."

" 25, " 14 " "lopped" read "topped."

" 33, " 7 " "nine" read "four to five."

" 40, " 4 " "cultivation" read "ventilation."

" 42, " 5 " "create" read "increase."

" 43, " 8 " "gentle undulated" read "gently un-
dulating."

" 43, " 9 " "sparely" read "sparsely."

" 49, " 14 " "and" read "of the."

THE

NATURE AND CULTIVATION
OF COFFEE.

CHAPTER I.

DESCRIPTION AND HISTORY.

BOTANISTS and historians are alike divided in opinion
as to the origin of the name of the plant; but it appears
probable that it was given from its being first found in
its natural wild state in the country of Cafe, one of the
provinces of Abyssinia, where at this day it is still
found in the woods, and where a large sheep-skinful
may be purchased for less than a shilling,* and where
it is called Kahwah. The plant itself belongs to the
natural order Cinchonacea, an order which supplies
many of the most useful drugs and medicines. There
are several species, but as opinions differ as to whether
some of these are not mere varieties, and as many of
the distinctive qualities yield to cultivation, and are
materially influenced by differences of soil, climate,

* Harris's "Highlands of Æthiopia."

1

and temperature, one only, the coffee of commerce, produced by the *Coffea Arabica,* will meet with notice in these pages. The plant is now widely diffused over all the tropical parts of the world. It is found in most of the West India Islands, in all the provinces of Central America, Cayenne, Brazil, Peru, and Bolivia. In Africa it has found a congenial habitat; in the rising colony of Natal, and again in the northern part of the same continent; it flourishes both in a wild and cultivated state in many parts of Nubia and Abyssinia; in Asia it is widely spread over Arabia, the western coast of India, Ceylon, Bourbon, Mauritius, Java, and some of the Pacific Islands; and in many of these places it is found in climates differing as much as 20° in average temperature. The coffee plant will bear extremes of climate better than most plants. In Jamaica it is found on the Blue Mountain, upwards of 6000 feet above the sea, and in the East Indies it is seen growing and producing at Coonoor on the Neilgherries at a similar elevation; whilst, on the other hand, it is also seen growing at the level of the sea, in both hemispheres, a difference of average temperature of from 20° to 30°. It is contended that the coffee produced at a high elevation is of a finer quality than that grown in a warmer temperature; this is, however, very questionable. No coffee yet produced bears a better character or realizes a higher price in the market than Cannon's Mysore; this is certainly not more than 3500 feet, and the coffee produced at the extremes of climate is always small, generally much lighter, and the actual number of berries far less than that grown in a genial climate. Experience has proved that from lat. 6° to 12° an elevation of from 3000 to 4000 feet is the most suited, whilst beyond this 500 feet of elevation should be allowed for every degree of latitude. It. is now an ascertained fact, that much of the far-famed Mocha coffee is produced in India and shipped from Bombay to Mocha, and no inconsiderable portion also comes from the low land of Cafe and Euarea in Africa. The excellence of Mocha coffee appears to exist more in the method of curing than from any other cause.

There is quite as much variance of opinion as to the facts of the discovery and use of coffee as a beverage, as there is regarding its nomenclature, the oft-repeated fable of the effect of the leaves being first discovered in goats which had been browsing on the leaves, would not account for the use of the roasted seed; whilst unfortunately for the propagators of this tale it is well known that no animal will eat the coffee leaf, cattle passing through an estate may take a few leaves as they pass, but fortunately for the planter the tree itself has few enemies, and estates are left without fence or hedge of any kind with impunity. Sambur, deer, bison, and wild hog, pass through estates without doing any injury, except occasionally rubbing their horns or antlers against the bushes, and perhaps tasting a few leaves. It appears most probable that as in almost every other case of human food, necessity was the mother of invention. The fruit itself is beautiful in appearance, and sweet and luscious to the taste, and when it was once discovered that it contained a bean, nothing would be more natural than that its use should be economized and various modes of cooking be attempted, until the present process had been found the most palatable. All accounts agree that it was first introduced into England from Turkey about the year 1650, but for many years its use was confined to the rich, and it was used as a stimulating liquor in place of wine. In 1690 the plant was introduced into Java, where it was kept by the Dutch with their usual jealousy, and it was not until about 1720 that it was imported into Surinam, another Dutch colony, and thence, some ten years after, its cultivation was attempted in Jamaica. It does not appear to have been introduced into Brazil until 1782, and thence it has become widely spread all over the tropical world, whilst from Brazil alone 1,495,697 bags, or 2,243,545 cwts., were exported in 1864, though the quantity has much decreased of late compared with previous years' exports.

CHAPTER II.

PRODUCTION AND CONSUMPTION.

THE Eastern hemisphere appears quite to have taken the place of the Western in the production and supply of coffee. Partly owing to the high price of labour and land, and partly to other causes, such as exhaustion of soil, etc., the British possessions in the West Indies only produce between three and four millions of pounds of coffee annually, against fully ten times that quantity twenty years ago. The French and Spanish colonies are also giving up the cultivation in favour of other articles, and the fall in the price of the article, together with the rise in the price of labour, provisions, and land, all over the world, has reduced the area where coffee can be profitably cultivated, to a very small extent. Brazil, Java, a portion of the Central American Republics, and our own colonies of Ceylon and British India, are the only countries where coffee can be cultivated with certainty as a profitable speculation. It has been already shown that the produce of the first of these has fallen off considerably of late years. In Jáva it is stationary and the produce is inferior, whilst in Ceylon it can be produced and shipped for 35s. per cwt., and in British India at one-sixth less, owing to the lower rate of wages and cheaper transport to the coast.

The total quantity of coffee consumed in Great Britain in 1864 was about thirty-five millions of pounds, of which nearly thirty millions was the produce of India and Ceylon. The total exports into Europe amount now to about 290,000,000 lb., and the consumption having of late years increased enormously on the Continent, as will be seen from the annexed table, a rise of price is imminent as soon as the States of America shall resume their former consumption. The following figures show the exports from England to the Continent :—

In 1859	.	.	8,600 tons
„ 1860	.	.	12,743 „
„ 1861	.	.	13,168 „
„ 1862	.	.	17,262 „
„ 1863	.	.	22,161 „

France alone consumes one-sixth of the total production of the world. In 1809 the exports from Jamaica alone exceeded 83,000,000 lb., whilst at present they do not reach 6,000,000 lb. In British Guiana the exports have fallen in like manner from 9,472,000 lb. to nothing, scarcely sufficient being now grown for consumption in the colony. In Porto Rico the production has slightly increased, but if we turn to Brazil we find the following results. The exports from Rio were in

1859	.	.	2,026,819 bags
1860	.	.	2,122,334 „
1861	.	.	2,040,810 „
1862	.	.	1,486,207 „
1863	.	.	1,312,902 „
1864	.	.	1,495,697 „

The shipments from Rio to the United States were in

1859	. .	1,149,441 bags
1860	. .	960,804 „
1861	. .	690,270 „
1862	. .	390,956 „
1863	. .	387,138 „
1864	. .	553,120 „

Showing a decrease in the exports from Rio to the United States of 734,650 cwts. per annum, and a decrease in the total production of Brazil of nearly 1,000,000 cwts. annually, or more than the total production of Ceylon and India, that of the former being about 800,000 cwts. in 1864, and of the latter less than 200,000 cwts. in the same year. In the current year an increase to the former of about 50,000 cwts., and to the latter of about the same quantity is expected, bringing the production up to the amount of the deficet from Brazil. From Costa Rica and Venezuela the exports have considerably increased of late years, and the quality of the coffee is good, though not equal to best Ceylon or Indian produce.

In Java coffee is a Government monopoly, and Government purchases the produce at a fixed price. The average produce is about 1,250,000 cwts. annually. The trade for the last five years is shown in the figures annexed.

Export of Coffee from Java.

1859	. .	59,789 tons
1860	. .	54,638 „
1861	. .	61,783 „
1862	. .	63,286 „
1863	. .	62,400 „

CHAPTER III.

As is often the case, theory is opposed to practice, in upholding the idea that there is any substantial difference in the coffee grown in different countries : where such difference is really found to exist, it will generally be the result of different modes of cultivation, and preparation for the market, or what is known as curing. If we take the product of the principal coffee-growing countries, we shall find them distinguished by the following characteristics. The West India coffee is for the most part even sized, pale and yellowish, firm and heavy, with a fine aroma, and losing little in weight by the roasting process. That from Brazil is larger, less solid, greenish or white, and the marketable article is usually styled by brokers as "low," or "low middling." Java coffee is smaller, slightly elongated, pale in colour, deficient in aroma and essential oil, and light. Ceylon produces coffee of all descriptions, but the ordinary plantation coffees are even, colour, slightly canoe-shaped, strong in aroma and flavour, of considerable gravity, and admit better of adulteration than most other kinds. Between Ceylon and Indian coffee there is little difference, the brokers state that Wynaad and Neilgherry coffee have generally the preference in the market ; but this may be ascribed partly to the small quantities of the latter in the market, and also to the planters in India having bestowed more care on the preparation in order to get a name. The quality of coffee is mainly dependent on the soil and general cultivation, and slightly on the climate, the quantity of rain being found to exercise a material effect on the quality of the crop, and a dry climate producing a better flavoured and more coloury bean than the excessive moisture prevalent on some of the most highly esteemed districts, both in the east and western hemispheres. It may be mentioned in proof of the first of these statements, that the size and appearance of the bean has been entirely changed by improved or neglected cultivation, and in one estate in India the beans are scarcely larger than sweet peas, owing to the proprietor having adopted a theory of never pruning the trees, whilst several estates in Wynaad and Ceylon, that had been neglected, have improved both in quality and quantity of produce to an extent scarcely credible, since they have been manured and pruned. Seeds from Mocha, Brazil, and Java, have been tried in Ceylon and India, and the produce has not differed in any respect from that of the plant already in existence there. A moist climate has further a tendency to produce long, weak, elongated shoots, drooping at the extremities, and the foliage is thin, the leaf long, but devoid of substance. The real Mocha coffee is cured in an entirely different mode from that practised in the colonies. The berries when ripe are picked, and spread out on large drying grounds, and are dried with the pulp and parchment on the bean; when thoroughly dry the berries are passed under wooden rollers or pounded in wooden mortars similar to those used for removing the husk from rice, and the outer skin being thus removed, the beans are winnowed, garbled, sized, and packed for the market. The coffee prepared in this way is seldom so even in colour and appearance, but the aroma and flavour is better. This method is, however, open to serious disadvantages. Owing to the much greater bulk of the coffee before the pulp is removed, the room for drying would require to be very extensive, and as coffee is very liable to ferment in the pulp, it must be laid very thin, and constantly turned; whilst in event of wet weather and exposure to moisture, or the equally dangerous alternative of heaping it up, the whole would ferment and be utterly spoiled. The system at present pursued by all European planters of removing the pulp by means of machinery, which will be hereafter described, as soon as the berries (or as they are called by planters, cherries) are picked, and thus placing the bean beyond the risk of fermentation, appears the best. The quality and colour of the bean is also materially affected by its treatment after the pulp is taken off. It should not be kept too long in the vats for the removal of the mucilage. This is a sweet sticky substance, between the outer rind and the parchment, which rapidly turns acid and loses its mucilaginous quality, and can be easily washed off after twelve hours' soaking in the vats; if allowed to remain too long on the bean, it will communicate an unpleasant flavour. After being washed and put out on the barbacues to dry, it is of importance to keep the coffee constantly turned until it is all surface dry, and the beans cease to adhere to each other, but it should not be exposed to sun and wind until the pellicle known as the parchment cracks, unless it is purposed at once to peel and pack it, as every hour's exposure to the atmosphere after that is removed takes away both from the colour and the aroma of the bean. For the same reason casks or cases are preferable to sacks for its conveyance to the market, and it cannot be too strongly impressed on the planter that coffee has a strong attraction for damp and for all scents, and will become thoroughly impregnated with any substance with which it is brought in contact. Pepper, ginger, salt fish, spirits of all kinds, and cocoa-nut oil, all impart their flavour and scent to coffee, and will spoil it if amongst the same cargo. In what has been said above, it is of course supposed that the coffee is picked when fully ripe, and not, as is frequently the case with native planters, that the trees are stripped directly a few berries are ripe on them, for no care in curing or packing will impart colour or flavour to a half-ripe bean. In order to obviate as much as possible the risk of loss of colour and aroma in the conveyance to Europe, it has been proposed to send the coffee home in the parchment skin, in the same state in which it is brought from the various estates to the shipping port to be cleaned and shipped, but although the actual weight of the parchment or refuse is only one-fifth of the whole, yet the greater expense of labour in this country has proved an insurmountable obstacle. As the expense of cleaning and shipping is £5 per ton on the coast, and all mechanical operations are performed with greater facility in this country, this objection may, it is hoped, be removed at some future time, especially as there is reason to believe that the parchment skin, though thrown away abroad, could be utilized here, both it and the pulp being used in Brazil and Arabia as inferior coffee.

CHAPTER IV.

THE object of the present work being to supply information to the coffee-grower, and to the very large number of the public who are in various ways connected with and interested in coffee-planting, it has not been thought necessary to enter upon a scientific analysis of the composition of the bean, or to enter into the chemical and physiological view of the subject. The part roasted is a hard horny albumen, and many other plants having seeds of the same texture are frequently used to adulterate it; the principal substitute, however, is chicory, and many persons prefer coffee with a small mixture of chicory in it. This is, however, purely a matter of taste; those who prefer really good coffee will buy it only from respectable grocers, and will, if able, roast it themselves. It may not be probably known that an apparatus was patented not long ago for making artificial coffee from chicory and other foreign matters. The mixture of coffee with chicory may always be detected by sprinkling it on the surface of water : genuine coffee floats a long time, and sinks slowly, colouring the water but slightly; chicory sinks quickly, and colours the water a deep brown at once. Horse beans, roasted corn, and various other substances are used to defraud the public, and if common report may be believed, even more objectionable substances, such as roasted horse liver and other animal matters, find their way into the coffee-pot to the profit of the grocer and the loss of the planter.

Attention has been lately drawn to the use of the leaf of the coffee tree as a substitute for tea, and experience has shown that a beverage prepared from coffee leaf is not only palatable, but is by some preferred to the best Pekoe or Souchong. There is little doubt that such tea would, moreover, command a sale in Europe, so that the process is reduced simply to a question of profit or loss in production. The first obvious objection is that it would injure the trees to deprive them of their leaves, which constitute their breathing organs, but on many estates where the trees are luxuriant and constant pruning required, no inconsiderable quantity might be collected from the shoots and suckers which are pruned off; this could, however, only be done at certain seasons when the pruning is being carried on, and practical experiment alone can prove whether the leaf at this season is at the fittest state for manufacture. The second objection is the cost of collecting and preparing the leaves ; this, however, applies equally to the cultivation of tea, and need not be considered of importance if it was ascertained that coffee-tea would realize the average price of Assam produce.

CHAPTER V.

COFFEE appears to have been first introduced into Ceylon by the Dutch, some time about 1690, but it was not until 1824 that coffee planting on a large scale was commenced by Sir Edward Barnes. The great increase in planting dates from 1835, since which year, with the exception of a pause owing to commercial depression, from 1847 to 1850, the cultivation has been annually increasing, and at present there are 265,000 acres owned by planters, of which about the half are under cultivation. In Ceylon, as in India, the coffee is found to succeed best at an elevation of from 2500 to 4500 feet. Below the former the tree suffers from droughts, and requires shade and irrigation, but where this last can be successfully practised the cultivation might be carried on as low as 1500 or 2000 feet. When a higher elevation than 4500 feet is selected, the trees suffer from the cold winds, the crop is late, and does not all ripen, part of it commonly dying on the trees, and the plants become woody and full of twigs, forming numbers of small shoots instead of expending their strength in blossom and fruit. The exports from Ceylon in 1864-5 are upwards of 800,000 cwts., and this quantity will probably be largely increased, as much of the land in cultivation is not yet bearing.

The railroad now in process of formation from Colombo to Kandy, and the immense benefits resulting from the successful operation of the road ordinance, in opening new roads, will much facilitate transport in Ceylon, and will impart additional impetus to the cultivation.

The effects of elevation may be stated to be, the lower parts produce much sooner and generally larger crops, but with some uncertainty, as they are more dependent on the seasons ; the estates on the higher ranges produce smaller but more steady crops, and seldom are in full bearing till the fifth year. It is frequently stated that the higher the elevation the finer the quality of the coffee, but this is very doubtful, and practical experience proves that the quality of the coffee is more influenced by cultivation than elevation, and even were it the case, it will be admitted by all that ten cwts. of coffee per acre at an average price more than compensates for the few shillings extra per cwt. on thirty to forty per cent. less produce.

Many circumstances, however, affect climate besides elevation. The neighbourhood of high mountain ranges generally attracts fog, cloud, and rain, and the base of large hills will be generally found moister and warmer than the same elevation some distance from the high land. It will be obvious that at a low elevation far more moisture is necessary than at a higher and colder atmosphere. At 2000 feet 80 to 100 inches more rain is necessary than at 4500 feet. Again, aspect has much to do with climate ; a southwesterly exposure being subject to high wind, hot sun (and the full force of the monsoon); whilst a north-east to a north-west will be sheltered from the direct rays of the sun during the dry season or summer solstice, and the heavy monsoon rains, which on the west coast of India or Ceylon set in from the south-west, will strike against the land at an acute angle, and lose much of the force from being unaccompanied with wind. To sum up briefly what has been said, high elevation with cold and wet, and exposure to high winds, or, on the other hand, a low range with excessive heat and drought, are alike unfavourable, and much judgment is needed in the selection of such a climate as shall possess a happy medium of these characteristics.

The subject of soil is, however, one more difficult of solution, and one that is likely to excite more debate than that of climate. All prefer a deep, loose mould, of a dark chocolate colour, but many denounce as utterly unfit for cultivation a soil possessing all these advantages, because it is covered with the secondary jungle (or as it is called in Ceylon, chenah; and in India, roomrie) which takes the place of the original forest, when this has been cut down to produce a crop of grain for the natives; others, again, decry soil, however rich, if it has had either fern or grass upon it; many object to the heavy bamboo land, now so much sought after, and so profitably cultivated in Southern India. Under the old system of coffee cultivation, which consisted simply of cutting down a mass of jungle, burning it off, planting the tree, and weeding once a month or once a year, as found most convenient, without any attempt at high cultivation or manuring, all these objections were well founded; but the modern system of manuring, pruning, and trenching is rapidly equalizing the value of all soils, and the principal object of the planter should be to select a deep and moderately loose soil, on such a slope as can be worked without danger of its being washed away, and not too far from roads or pasture. The means of access to high roads is a point of great importance affecting the estate in the expenses of every department, and always determining the serious item of transport of crop from the estate.

CHAPTER VI.

FROM what has been said in the last chapter, it will be evident that too much care and trouble can scarcely be taken in the selection of suitable land in the first instance.

Several most important qualifications are necessary, the absence of any one of which may neutralize the others. Perhaps the majority of planters will agree that the salubrity of the proposed scene of operations is one of the most important considerations; and next is an elevation and climate suitable for the plant—both these essentials being almost beyond the power of art to remedy. Land of a gentle slope and proper aspect, and on which a system of high cultivation, such as manuring, trenching, and irrigation, if necessary, can be practised, is also of the utmost importance; whilst a good deep soil of tolerable quality, and capable of improvement by ordinary cultivation, is also a *sine quâ non*. Of less consequence, but by no means to be overlooked, is the point of distance from towns and villages from whence labour can be procured, and the means of access and egress from the estate should also be considered.

The several operations comprised under the one head, "Opening an Estate," are—1. Formation of nurseries; 2. Felling and clearing; 3. Marking roads; 4. Lining and pitting; 5. Filling pits and planting; 6. Buildings.

1. Formation of nurseries. This should generally be done at least six months previous to the commencement of the clearing. The felling and clearing is usually begun at the commencement of the dry season, in October; the nurseries should therefore be made in the previous May or June, a tolerably level site being selected. The soil should be trenched at least a foot deep, and after being well pulverized, and all roots and stones removed, should be laid out in beds four feet wide; and after being copiously manured, or well covered with ashes, planted either with seeds four inches apart, or with young seedlings brought from the nearest estate, at about six inches apart in the rows, and four inches distance each row. This latter is by far the most economical, both in time and money —the seedling is much more certain to come on well than a seed; and as it is probably three or four months old when transplanted, this portion of its growth is saved to the planter. By the process of transplanting also the plant forms a number of fibrous roots, which enable it to bear the subsequent removal to its permanent place in the plantation. Should seeds be sown, it will be necessary to transplant them when about four inches high into other beds. A slight shade is generally of service for a few weeks after the nurseries have all been planted, but every particle of shade should be removed three or four months before it is intended to plant out. For the information of beginners, it may be stated that a bushel of cherry

coffee-seed will usually produce about 25,000 plants; a bushel of fresh parchment coffee, which is preferable to cherry, will produce about double that quantity; and an acre of nursery will hold 290,000 plants, planted six inches by four, or about 20,000 less when allowance is made for paths between the beds, etc.

2. Felling and clearing are easy operations when virgin forest is dealt with, but are tedious when tangled thickets of bamboo, or other thorny bushes, are prevalent. The smaller growth is generally cut first with billhooks, and this is frequently performed by women and boys; the able-bodied axemen next follow, cutting the trees nearly through, and then felling a tree of larger dimensions, so as to fall on what is notched; it brings all down in one mass. In heavy, thick forest, several acres are frequently brought down together; but in gentle slopes, and in thinly-wooded land, each tree has to be cut through separately. It will frequently occur that staging has to be erected round the trunks of some of the giants of the forest, as their projecting roots and buttresses prevent access to the real trunk. The forest, of whatever kind, being felled, has next to be lopped, so as to lie compactly, and to ensure a good burn, which usually takes place six weeks or two months after the felling. A bad burn is the cause of much expense in subsequent heaping and burning, and attention should therefore be paid to this operation.

3. Marking the roads. This should always be done as soon as possible, and all the trees which are lying across the line of roads should be turned off before the lining commences. The time · both of

superintendents and men will be economized by partial
formation of the roads before the other work is commenced, leaving them to be completed when there is
spare labour on the estate.

4. Lining and pitting. The distances usually
observed for planting coffee are six feet by six feet or
six feet by five feet. Close planting is serviceable in
hindering the growth of the weeds, and in enabling
the plants to shelter each other from the effect of high
winds; and of course the extra number of plants to
the acre are followed, in the first two crops, by pro-
portionate increase of produce. Having, therefore,
fixed on the distance to be observed, the easiest
method is to mark off a cross in the centre of each
field, and proceeding from the centre with a line with
marks at the proper distances for the spaces between
the stakes. The ends being held at equal distances
from the last stakes, are put in by boys at the mark on
the line. Trifling inaccuracies must happen in consequence of the irregularity of the land, but the only
method to avoid these would be by irregularly extending the distance between the plants, sometimes to
eight and nine feet; and on the whole the plan is as
good as can be followed. At the distance of six feet
by six feet, an acre will contain about 1200 plants, but
the space occupied by roads, rocks, stumps, etc., will
probably curtail this amount about ten per cent.—
stakes being put in to mark the places where the pits
are to be made ; these are generally dug by contract,
and it may be useful to know that, in ordinary forest
soil, with an average amount of stones and roots,
thirty pits, twenty inches wide by eighteen inches

deep, is fair work for a man for a day, at a cost in India of sixpence to eightpence, and in Ceylon of from ninepence to one shilling. Crowbars with one end widened to about three inches, and short, thick hoes or momaties to remove the loosened soil, are the most useful tools for this work. It is of some importance to consider beforehand what is the nature of the cultivation to be followed, because, if it is purposed to trench over the whole of the ground immediately, large pits are not requisite, but they may be made deep and narrow; if, on the other hand, the process of trenching is to be deferred, even two feet wide and two deep is not too large, and anything less than this would be false economy.

5. Filling pits and planting. If the felling and clearing has been accomplished in good time, the land will have been ready for lining and pitting in February, and the pits will consequently be open for three or four months before the rains set in, and the work of planting commences. They will be much improved by this exposure to rain and atmospheric influence, and it will probably occur to the planter to fill up the pits with the surface soil taken from the spaces between the pits, leaving that taken out of the pits to be improved by exposure. The practice of filling the pits after very heavy rain, when the pits are half-full of water, is very objectionable, as the soil cakes into a hard mass. Care should be taken, if possible, to have the pits filled a day or two before planting, as the soil is then cooler and more settled.

We now arrive at the most important item in the first year's operations—Planting. Plants from the nursery, stumps, and seedlings, are alike used in forming plantations. The first are preferable reared in nurseries, as already shown. Until they are twelve or fifteen inches high, with one or two pair of primary branches, they should be taken up with a ball of earth whenever practicable ; but where the distance from the nursery to the planting ground precludes this mode, the roots may be dipped into a mixture of cow-dung and earth, to prevent the action of the wind and air on the fine fibrous roots, and thus guarded, they can be carried for miles. Extreme care is necessary in planting not to turn the roots up ; the safest plan is to lower the tree into the place made for its reception rather deeper than it is intended to remain, and throwing a little loose soil on the roots, to draw the plant up to the proper level ; by this means, all the roots will be pointing downwards, and doubling up the tap root will be prevented. The earth should be trodden round the plant, to prevent its being shaken by the wind ; and it should never be buried below the crown of the root, as the upper bark is liable to rot off if covered over with earth, and the plant in consequence perishes. Stumps, which are neither more nor less than older plants cut down two inches from the ground, may be planted with less risk even when the weather is dry and the season more advanced. In ordinary seasons, a number of buds or suckers make their appearance on the stump within a month of its being planted ; these should all be rubbed off, except the lowest one, and this will in a short time grow up, and throw out lateral branches, exactly like a nursery plant. Stumps generally bear a little earlier, probably because they are usually made from very old nurseries.* Plants, indeed, which are too old to plant out in the ordinary way make excellent stumps.† The plants once put in, the roads previously marked and traced out should be completed, and the estate should be weeded, and from the day the coffee-trees are put in no other green.leaf should be seen in the estate, but every weed should be pulled up before it is three inches high. If this plan be pursued, the subsequent cultivation will require very few hands, and the cost of weeding will not be one quarter that incurred if the weeds are once allowed to seed on the estate. When the plants are about two years old, they will require to be lopped—*i.e.*, the leading stem or shoot to be cut off. The height at which this should be done must depend on several circumstances; if entirely neglected, the trees are apt to become weak, tall bushes, with irregular side-branches or primaries; and in exposed, windy situations they will be much shaken and broken by the wind. The common practice is to keep the trees at about four feet in height, but even this is too high, unless the soil is very good and the situation sheltered; three feet, or even two feet six inches, will be found better in the majority of cases.

The objects gained by topping are to keep the tree

* Some planters cut down the plants in the nurseries, or "stump" them, a month before they are required to plant out, and they will then have acquired a second stem or sucker, before being planted out; but the plan is not to be recommended, as the young tender shoot is very liable to damage in transplanting.

† It may not be generally known that coffee propagates readily by cuttings; but if the cutting be taken from one of the side-branches, it will never form a centre stem, but will always evince the peculiar characteristics of the lateral branches; but if, on the other hand, a sucker or shoot be planted, it will form a plant perfect in all respects and in no way to be distinguished from a seedling.

to such an height that the fruit can be conveniently gathered, and that pruning, etc., can be easily performed, and further to throw the strength of the plant into the fruit-producing branches, which by this means spread rapidly on each side and shelter each other, whilst they shade the ground and check the growth of weeds. Some planters advocate the trees being left tall until six or eight inches can be taken off, necessitating cutting into the formed wood, where at the same time they remove one of each of the primary branches, about an inch from the main stem, leaving an unseemly fork projecting four or six inches above the growing plant, the object of this being, as they maintain, to form such a callosity, or knot, above the producing branches, as will prevent the weight of the fruit tearing the branches apart, and splitting the main stem ; but it is very doubtful whether this object is attained, as the portion of stem thus left is a fruitful source of annoyance in sending out suckers from the joint where the two primaries have been removed, and as soon as it ceases, the fork being deprived of all circulating sap, gradually dries up and decays down to the growing wood, rendering the tree more liable than before to the accident it was sought to guard against. A better plan appears to top the trees early, in the green sappy shoot, before it has become lignine, or fibrous, immediately above a pair of growing primaries. By this means there is no joint left above to form buds and shoots, and the top gradually forms into a knot, or callosity, sufficiently tough to withstand the weight on each side of the tree. It must always be borne in mind that a coffee-tree cannot replace a primary branch; but it always replaces a maiden stem if lost, by a vigorous sucker, and many old worn out estates have been completely renovated by cutting down the trees two inches from the ground, and allowing a good shoot to proceed from the stump and take the place of the tree thus decapitated, due regard at the same time being paid to improvement of the soil, etc. The shoot thus left will bear a small crop in two years, and a full crop in the third and fourth, so that only one and a half crop is lost by thus cutting down an estate; and with estates which have been much neglected in pruning, etc., and have in consequence lost many of their primaries, this will be found by far the most satisfactory method of renovation, as a property thus treated will present all the appearance and regularity of a young and flourishing estate.

In the course of the second year it will be necessary to fill up all the vacancies in the first year's planting-out from deaths and omissions. This is usually called supplying, and should be done with great care, as the neat appearance of the estate much depends on the regularity of the plants; and the vacancies, until timely filled up, will become nurseries for weeds, thus increasing the labour besides diminishing the produce of the estate. It will be found a good plan to grow a number of plants in large bamboos cut so as to form a flower-pot, and to use these in filling up the gaps, as all chance of failure is thus prevented. The plants need not be turned out of the bamboos, but the bamboo-pot should be cracked on one side, and the whole may be then buried, as it will soon rot and be consumed by grubs, etc.

CHAPTER VII.

THE erection of suitable buildings is scarcely less important than the opening and planting the estate, for although they are neither large nor expensive, yet much of the health and comfort of the superintendent and coolies will depend on the sites chosen for their abodes; and the economical working of the estate will be greatly dependent on the situation of the pulping-house and store. It will probably be found necessary to run up temporary lines, or coolie-huts, on the nearest clear spot, before commencing any work; but as a rule, only permanent and substantial buildings should be erected. They will be found much the most economical in the end, and give much more satisfaction whilst they are in existence.

The situation for the superintendent's house will be selected with a view to health and general accessibility, and should be placed on a site commanding a good view of the estate, and if possible of the store and pulping-house; but on no account too near these last, the noise of the pulping machinery and coolies, and the effluvium from the drying coffee and fermenting pulp, being very disagreeable.

The pulping-house and store should be placed in a central spot, easy of access from all parts of the estate, and the point of transport of coffee, either by bullocks or carts from the store, should also be taken into consideration.

It is, of course, understood that a small stream of water is absolutely necessary at the pulping-house, to pulp and wash the coffee, and should large works or water-wheels be contemplated, the position will be mainly determined by its capabilities in this respect; desirable, however, as it is to secure the assistance of water for the machinery, it is not often that this can be attained without sacrificing equally important advantages, and instances are not unfrequent of the works being placed in inaccessible situations, simply to secure water privileges, although the assistance so derived was more than counterbalanced by the expense and inconvenience of extra carriage of the crop both before and after pulping.

The coolie lines will generally be placed as near the scene of their operations as possible, due regard at the same time being had to the health of the people, and access to water for their requirements.

The coffee-berry when gathered from the tree is the colour and shape of a ripe damson, for although it may be considered ripe when red, it will benefit by remaining on the tree until it has passed into damson colour. If the berry is squeezed, two coffee-beans are found, covered with a thin skin exactly resembling parchment, between which and the outer rind there is a very sweet mucilaginous fluid, already alluded to.

The operation called pulping is removing this outer cherry rind and washing off the mucilage, leaving the bean in the parchment skin, in which it is dried and conveyed to the shipping port. The machine called the pulper passes the cherry between a barrel covered with perforated copper, something like a very large nutmeg grater, and an iron bar or chop, the distance of which is adjusted by means of spiral screws, so as to insure the bean's being pressed against the barrel, but yet not so close for the inner bean to be cut or pricked. The difference of size in the coffee renders this seemingly simple operation one of considerable difficulty, for if the chop is set too close, the larger berries will be crushed, whilst if adjusted to pulp the large coffee only, the smaller berries will pass through unpulped. As at present manufactured, coffee-pulpers are most unsatisfactory machines; but the usual plan pursued is to set the chop to pulp the larger coffee, and either to have another pulper for pulping the lesser berries, or to return the smaller passed berries to the feeding-trough or chopper, tightening the chop at the same time. Much the best machine yet invented is the disk pulper, patented by Messrs. Walker, of Kandy, Ceylon. The coffee passed through this is much less cut than by any other, and will average a higher price in sale. The coffee, after passing through the pulper, is passed on to a cistern, all the pulp, or, as it is called by planters, the tails, coming out at the back of the machine and remaining behind. After twelve hours' soaking, accompanied by slight fermentation, which decomposes the mucilage and facilitates its removal, the beans in the parchment are washed clean and put out on barbacues, or drying-grounds, to dry. These last are sometimes laid in brick and lime or covered with asphalte; more commonly, they are long platforms about three feet wide, on which is laid coir matting, which admits the escape of the moisture easily and hastens the drying process. Two or three days' exposure usually suffices to prepare the coffee for transport to the coast, which is variously effected, according to the means at the planter's disposal. Generally in Ceylon and India two-wheeled carts or pack bullocks are employed, which carry four to six bushels, in two sacks or gunny-bags, the driver having the coffee measured to him on the estate, and receiving a certain rate per bushel on delivery on the coast. Not only is this mode of carriage most precarious, but it is very expensive, the average paid by coffee estates in Ceylon for carriage of a bushel of parchment to the coast being about two shillings. In Southern India sixpence to ninepence is the average, but there many estates have the advantage of water carriage. Before leaving the subject of pulping, it may be remarked that it is always necessary to pulp the berries within twelve hours of their being picked, and that if they are at all dry on one side, as is often the case with the latter part of the crop, they will not pulp clean, but will either be crushed or pass out with unpulped coffee, and it will frequently be necessary to pass the coffee, as it comes from the pulpers, through sieves, to remove all the tails which come out on the wrong side, as these considerably retard the drying of the coffee and impart a bad colour to it.

To sum up briefly, it is requisite that the coffee berries should be quite ripe; that they should be pulped soon after being picked; that they are not cut or pricked in pulping; that the parchment coffee should not be too long in the cisterns ; and that it should be cleaned, washed, and then surface dried, as soon as practicable. The subsequent operations of peeling, garbling, sizing, and packing are generally performed at the shipping port, and will be considered in another chapter.

CHAPTER VIII.

PEELING, GARBLING, SIZING, AND PACKING FOR EXPORT.

THESE several operations are generally out of the planter's control, and are performed by the agents at the shipping port, who frequently purchase the coffee in the parchment, or undertake to deliver it upon ship at a given rate per ton. The average selling price of coffee in parchment at Colombo, or on the coast of India, is 60s. per cwt. of nine bushels; and the charges of peeling, sizing, garbling, packing in cases, and shipping are £5 per ton. There are several large establishments at Colombo, in Ceylon, and at Telli-cherry, Calicut, and Mangalore, in India, for the preparation of coffee for shipment, some employing two to three thousand hands daily. The machinery by which the parchment is removed is called a peeling-mill; it consists of two wheels of solid heavy wood, shod with sheet copper; these work in a circular trough thirty or thirty-six feet in diameter, and are generally turned by four men. This breaks the parch-ment skin, the coffee is then winnowed, and if care has been taken in curing the coffee, the whole of the parchment and silver skin will be removed, and the coffee will present a clean horny appearance. It is now garbled, as it is called, or examined by women who pick out all discoloured beans, and it is then

passed through cylinders or sieves made of perforated
zinc or wire, by which it is separated into different
sizes, the pea-berry, which is nearly round, being
separated by a peculiar rolling motion, either in the
sieves or by hand labour in baskets. The coffee is
now packed either in bags containing 1 cwt. each, or
in cases containing about 2½ cwts., or in casks containing 6 to 10 cwts., and is shipped. Of the modes
of package, casks are undoubtedly preferable; but as
these are not always obtainable, cases are frequently
used. Bags should only be used for inferior coffee,
triage, etc., as it is much more liable to damage in
bags than in cases or casks. Triage is the broken
coffee, with which commonly all the very small and
discoloured coffee is also mixed. It is of importance
that the wood of which the cases or casks are made
should be well seasoned, and it is advisable to char
them slightly inside by burning straw or shavings
inside them, the object being to prevent any contami-
nation of the coffee by the oil or gum in the wood.

CHAPTER IX.

COFFEE IN SOUTHERN INDIA.

THE similarity in the seasons and general physical character of the two countries, renders the practice and mode of cultivation in India similar to that in Ceylon. The south-east monsoon generally sets in fifteen or twenty days sooner in Ceylon than in India, which occasions the crops there to be earlier; and hence it follows that, though the crops are seldom picking in India before the 15th of October, and more commonly a month later, in Ceylon it is commenced as early as August on some estates. There is a disadvantage attending early crops in the prevalence of rain up to the end of November, and, from what has been already said, it will be gathered that fine weather considerably assists crop work; in fact, without it artificial means must be resorted to for drying the coffee, or it would either ferment or become mouldy. To those planters as are so unfortunately situated as to have estates which ripen their crops in the rainy season, an apparatus patented by Mr. Clerihew, and exhibited at the International Exhibition in 1851, may be confidently recommended. It is too complex to be understood without diagrams and plans, for which there is not space in this work. Suffice it to say, that the rationale of the process is to draw a draft of

heated air from a furnace through the damp coffee,
and to drive it off when saturated by the means of
powerful ventilators.   .

There are at present over 120 coffee estates in
Wynaad, about 50 in Coorg and Nuggur, and 20 on
the Neilgherries, and between 30 and 40 in other
parts of India. Unfortunately we have no reliable
data as to the latter, the cultivation being widely
distributed over various ranges of hills, but the aggre-
gate cultivation in these parts is about 2000 acres.
In Wynaad there are about 75,000 acres occupied for
estates, of which 32,000 are in cultivation. In Coorg
and Mysore a little over 30,000 acres have been taken
up, of which scarcely one-third is yet in cultivation ;
and on the Neilgherries the cultivated area is under
2000 acres. In 1865, the exports from India were
22,400,000 lb., but a very large portion of the produce is retained for home consumption. The average
yield of coffee in Wynaad is slightly above that in
Ceylon, according to the statistics furnished by the
Ceylon Planters' Association ; the average of the
former being about 8 cwts. per acre against 6 cwts. in
the latter. In both countries, however, estates are to
be found which have yielded 18 to 20 cwts. an acre
under good cultivation. It is not the intention, in
the present work, to enter into a comparison of the
relative advantages of each country for the growth of
coffee, but simply to present facts to the reader's
notice, leaving him to form his own opinion. The
actual routine of cultivation is the same in both
countries. The system of pruning is, perhaps, better
understood and practised in Ceylon than in India ;

more care is also taken to keep the estates clean, but cattle do not thrive in Ceylon, and manure, being procured with difficulty, is not often applied. The planters are more favourably situated with regard to roads, police, and general executive administration in Ceylon than in India; this fact arising probably from their different status in the two countries. In Ceylon the planting community are influential men, forming a large body of the tax-paying class; their produce is the chief article of export, exceeding in value two millions yearly; their interests are represented in the Council by their own delegate, and special legislation has been put in force for their benefit. Until lately, members of both branches of the services engaged in the pursuit, and interested themselves in forwarding the interests of the planters, and from the Governor downwards scarcely a man in the colony, but was in some measure connected with the fascinating speculation; and although the connection of Government servants with commercial pursuits is now forbidden, the spirit that was then awakened has not slumbered, and planters are recognized as worthy the encouragement and protection of the Legislature.

In India, unfortunately, the old exclusive spirit, which would govern "India for the services," has not yet become extinct. The most obvious reforms are urged in vain. Except in some few districts, the planter experiences much difficulty even in procuring possession of and title to land. The most incompetent members of the services are frequently deputed to the charge of the districts where the unlucky Europeans most congregate, and every representation and request

for legal reform and redress is met with the hack-
neyed old conventionality respecting class legislation, etc. The state of the roads, police, and magis-
terial jurisdiction in most of the districts, settled by
Europeans, are by no means creditable to the executive
administration of the country; and until the European
is accorded in India that justice and protection he
meets in other colonies, they form a serious drawback
to the advantages presented in other respects by cheap
and abundant labour, and the lower price of land.

CHAPTER X.

ORDINARY cultivation consists in careful weeding, never allowing a weed to be three inches high, in removal of the suckers, and gourmand shoots, and in taking off all secondary shoots on the primaries within three inches of the stem, and then allowing them at only regular distances of two to three inches apart, with a regular succession of young wood coming on; the fruit is produced on one-year old wood, although in some favoured districts, branches two or three years old are seen covered with berries. It will generally be found that rather dry climates favour this mode of bearing, indeed, the excessive moisture prevalent in many of the most esteemed districts, is very adverse to the production of heavy crops. It is, therefore, difficult to lay down any positive rules for side pruning, as it is evident that this must be influenced by the nature of the climate. In a dry temperature, with little fog or supercumbent moisture, the trees may be allowed to produce much more wood than can be permitted in very damp situations, where every glimpse of sunshine is required, and where too great luxuriance, in this respect, will be followed by the appearance of what is called rot. This is simply the leaves and fruit turning black and falling off before they are matured, followed frequently by the decay of the shoots, and in some cases by death of the tree, the cause being evidently too much moisture and lack of cultivation; the remedy, therefore, is obvious. Planters are still divided both in opinion and practice on the subject of weeding. On some estates it is only practised twice a year, the tall rampant weeds being cut once or twice in the interim with sickles, and the land being only hoed over once before and once after crop, but the majority of experienced cultivators endeavour to keep their estates perfectly clean, hoeing up the weeds not less seldom than once in two months, and then burying both weeds and pruning between the coffee bushes.

The practice of manuring is of late years attracting considerable attention. In former years when land was comparatively cheap, and labour abundant, it was not thought worth while to work up estates, but as soon as the crops declined below the average, fresh virgin forests were felled and the old cultivation abandoned. The increased value of land, however, and the great expense now attending fresh clearing and planting, causes more attention to be paid to the up-keep of the land in cultivation, and small cultivated estates are more desired than large tracts yielding but little and comparatively worthless. Manure, as the most powerful agent in increasing the produce, requires every attention, and notwithstanding any goodness of soil should always be provided. With care much may be done on the estate to provide this requisite, in the shape of the decomposed pulp, wood ashes, decaying heaps of grass and weeds, and in many cases by the

utilization of the soil from marshes, which not unfrequently are found in the vicinity of estates, and which
when the lands surrounding them are covered with rich
vegetation, contain vegetable substances of the most
fertilizing character. From an analysis of the ash of
the coffee bean, we shall find that ordinary wood ashes
with a small quantity of phosphate of lime contain all
the essential constituents necessary for the production
of coffee. This easily procured stimulant, should always,
therefore, form a large portion of any manure which
may be applied. A compost unequalled in its effects
may be made, by mixing coffee pulp, wood ashes and
common salt with a large quantity of straw, weeds,
grass, or other vegetable matter, and applying them
when thoroughly decomposed.   Mr. Perindorge, of
Ceylon, recommended large quantities of manure,
being formed by saturating heaps of weeds, forest
leaves, etc., with repeated waterings of sal ammoniac,
and a cheap and economical method will be found to
cover each day's pulp, during the pulping season, with
a layer of vegetable rubbish of any kind, adding a thin
layer of mould or wood ashes, and watering it frequently
with salt water.   Where pasture is obtainable, cattle
manure will be found both cheap and efficacious, but it
must be borne in mind, that when cattle are fed only
on the grass found in jungle pasture, the nitrogenous
elements which render animal excrement of every kind
so valuable, are absent, and with the exception of a
small quantity of ammonia and of phosphoric acid,
every constituent of such manure will be found in
ordinarily decomposed vegetable matter. To render
cattle manure of its full value, it should be mixed with

ashes, bone dust, or other alkali, and it is scarcely necessary to remark that it is highly advisable that the cattle pens should be regularly littered down with dry grass, or other refuse, to absorb the liquid manure, and to create the quantity. It is urged by some that the latter is of equal value, when decomposed outside the cattle pen, and that spreading it in the shed only adds to the labour of cleaning out the sheds, without really benefiting the manure made, but it will be found that not only is the grass or straw more readily decomposed by being trodden down, but at the same time, as already shown, it imbibes the most valuable part of the manure, and fixes the volatile salts contained in it.

The ordinary phosphate of lime sold in England by the numerous patent manure manufacturers, is a very valuable compost, and may always be used with advantage, although the cost in some situations is almost prohibitory. Whilst all estates can be and, indeed, must be manured in some way or other to ensure their continued fruitfulness, the practice of trenching or digging over the whole estate can only be carried out in favourable localities, but where properly performed, it will in a great measure obviate the necessity of any extraneous application, and will materially decrease the labour of weeding.

It will be obvious that it is almost impossible to trench the side of steep rocky hills, or of heavy forest land, strewed with large trunks, and encumbered with large roots and stumps; fortunately, however, these are not the descriptions of soil which most need and most benefit by this operation. The soil amongst large rocks, or with loose superficial stones, is seldom hard or bound, and where heavy forest has existed, and the land is much encumbered with roots and stumps, the gradual decay of these loosen the soil and enable the coffee roots to penetrate in all directions. There is, however, a description of land, which until lately, was rejected by the majority of planters, but which has of late been found extremely productive, and this is what is known as bamboo land, or gentle undulated slopes sparely covered with large trees and bamboo thickets, the soil being generally heavy, and deep, but hard, and bound, and very full of grass seeds and other weeds. This land is generally inexpensive to clear, and is easily pitted, but it is absolutely necessary that it should be trenched over, at least twelve inches deep, both to enable the roots of the coffee trees to get abroad, and to eradicate the numerous weeds, which have perennial roots, and which would render the usual work of weeding almost ruinous, but where this operation is well done, and the soil is satisfactory, land so cultivated will be found, both more productive and more easily kept up than what is commonly known as forest land; and moreover, land thus treated will stand long drought, and produce more steady crops than estates cultivated on what may be called the old system. The routine of cultivation somewhat differs in this land, from what has been indicated above; the land after being felled and cleared, should be trenched over at once with mattocks, about six inches deep, it should then be lined and pitted, and much narrower pits may be permitted, than in land which is not trenched. Directly after the coffee plants are planted, it should be trenched over again to the depth of twelve inches, and if it has been trenched once before, as here advised, and the rain and air thus allowed to penetrate, the second trenching will be scarcely more expensive than weeding. Subsequent operations will consist in trenching over the whole of the land, burying all weeds, pruning, etc., once every year, a process which will frequently obviate the necessity for manure, and will materially lesson the labour of weeding.

It will doubtless occur to the practical agriculturist to time the annual trenching so as to bury a crop of growing weeds in the operation, and thus save one weeding, and at the same time enrich the soil. The months of May and June will be found the best for this work, or at the close of the rains in October and November, care must of course be taken to have efficient drains across the water shed, to prevent the soil when thus loosened, being carried away by the heavy rains. The practice of irrigation, wherever it can be followed, is not of less importance than that already advocated of trenching. On many estates there exists ample facility for its adoption, in the streams usually abundant in the mountain regions where coffee is generally cultivated, and its excellent effects will soon be visible in the assistance afforded to the plants in withstanding every drought, and in maturing heavy crops of fruit, which would not otherwise be brought to perfection. As a rule it will increase the productive qualities of estates twenty-five per cent, but in many low hot localities it will produce heavy crops, where otherwise, little or none could be obtained, as has been the case in the far-famed old Rajawelle Estate, in Ceylon.

Picking the crop is usually performed by women and children, as they can pick quite as much as an able-bodied man, or it is done by contract, when all hands are set to it and receive a given rate per bushel. In Southern India the average paid for picking is three pence to four pence per bushel, making the charges for one cwt., under this head, three shillings to four shillings. On old estates with a ripe crop of eight to twelve cwts. per acre on them, an expert picker will gather as much as six bushels in ten hours, but the average throughout the season, on ordinary estates, does not exceed two bushels. Bags should always be provided for the purpose of containing the ripe coffee cherries, and for carrying them to the store, as baskets are very liable to be upset, and stones and refuse may be picked up with the scattered fruit, which will damage the pulpers. The inefficiency of most of the machinery, at present in use for coffee pulping, has been already noticed. One of Walker's double disc pulpers will pulp fifty bushels per hour, with the labour of six men in a properly constructed pulping house, and other pulpers will do nearly as much, but at a considerable sacrifice of coffee, as most of these machines cut from five to ten per cent of the beans. Considerable ingenuity may be exercised in erecting the buildings so as to economize labour. The pulpers should be so placed that there is ample room for the washing vats or cisterns, without carriage of the coffee from one vat to another by manual labour, and a ready egress for the tails or pulp of the coffee should be provided by which it can be conveyed some distance from the pulping house and works. The situation of the store should also be contiguous to, and if practicable lower than the pulping house; above all both should be some distance from the Cooly lines or superintendent's bungalow, the effluvium from the rotting pulp and drying coffee being most offensive and very prejudicial to health. As already remarked, the pulp forms with other materials, a very fertilizing manure, and the water that has been used for pulping and washing the coffee, is of value for purposes of irrigation, but if applied in excess, is too stimulating and will kill vegetation.

Two hundred bushels of cherry coffee will generally produce 92 to 95 bushels of dried parchment, which will again turn out about one ton of marketable coffee. there is a slight difference between the coffee on different estates, and even the produce of the same estate in different seasons, or in the beginning and end of the same season; but the above will be found to be a safe average, and of the out-turn in parchment, one half in bulk and one-fifth in weight consists of the parchment bulk, the average weight of a bushel of clean coffee being 26 lb. Of coffee dried in the pulp, or dry cherry coffee as it is called, 120 bushels will usually make a ton of marketable produce, the expense of peeling and cleaning this are about 10 per cent. more than for parchment coffee.

A very useful form of monthly account will be found appended. It may be kept on either quarto or foolscap size, the latter perhaps is preferable. Three forms of daily journal are also shown, which will be found of great utility in enabling the superintendent and proprietor to calculate accurately the cost of each item of labour.

CHAPTER XI.

It will doubtless be expected that some estimate should be here given of the cost of opening and subsequently cultivating coffee estates. It must be evident however, that this is entirely dependent on the rates of wages, which differ materially in different countries, and which vary even in the different districts of Ceylon and of Southern India. The number of hands requisite for the different descriptions of work will be given with the average cost in Wynaad and Coorg.

Works.	Hands.	Cost per acre.
		£ s. d.
Clearing heavy forest	. 30	. 0 15 0
Lopping and burning off	. 10	. 0 5 0
Lining and pitting	. 50	. 1 5 0
Filling pits and planting	. 10	. 0 5 0
Roads . .	. 40	. 1 0 0
Trenching six inches deep	. 50	. 1 5 0
Do. twelve do.	. 50	. 1 5 0
		6 0 0

To this should be added the costs of
plants . . . 1 0 0
And an average for tools per acre of . 0 10 0

Carried forward . 7 10 0

	£	s.	d.
Brought forward .	7	10	0
Also of buildings . .	2	0	0
Superintendence . .	2	0	0
Medicine, stationery, extras .	0	10	0
Contingencies . . .	0	10	0
	12	10	0

Making the cost of planting the first year £12 10s. per acre.

The annual cultivation expenses on the same data will be as follows :—

	£	s.	d.
Weeding . . .	2	8	0
Nurseries and filling vacancies .	0	6	0
Pruning and handling . .	0	12	0
Manuring . . .	1	4	0
Postages, stationery, medicines, etc. .	0	10	0
Repair and wear of tools . .	0	5	0
Superintendence . .	1	10	0
Ordinary repair of buildings .	0	10	0
Contingencies . . .	0	5	0
	7	10	0

Bringing the annual cost of cultivation to £7 10s. per acre.

To this should be added the cost of coffee store, pulping house, pulpers, barbacues, etc., which for an estate of about 200 acres, would average £4 per acre, making the cost of an estate of above-named extent £39 per acre at the end of the third year, by which time a sufficient crop to pay further expenses may be expected. In many situations the original price of the land, and cost of making roads from the estate to the public road, will form a further charge, and without considering the first of these, which vary with every estate, according to the title under which it is held, the latter will probably bring the net cost per acre up to £40.

For a smaller estate than here estimated for, the cost would be proportionably less only in some items; in many, such as superintendence, general extras and ordinary buildings, the requirements of an estate of 100 acres, are scarcely less than for one of double that size.

The value and crop on an estate may fairly be estimated at 50s. per cwt. on the trees, the average charges on which will be as follows :—

	£	s.	d.
Picking, carriage, etc., per cwt. of ten bushels	0	4	0
Pulping and general charges	0	0	6
Carriage to the port	0	4	0
Preparation charges and shipping	0	5	0
Extras, superintendence, wear of bags, etc., etc.	0	1	6
Making for crop expenses a total of	0	15	0

per cwt., and as the best Ceylon and Indian coffee have averaged 78s. to 80s. per cwt., an ample margin is left for home expenses.

Assuming however, the value of the crops on the trees at 50s. per cwt., it will be seen that as already advanced it requires an average crop of three cwts. per

4

acre to defray the ordinary cultivation expenses, and that an estate can only be profitable when it yields above that quantity, and that its intrinsic value depends solely on the amount it produces above this ratio. It not unfrequently occurs that inexperienced parties become possessed of estates that are really worse than useless because they have not been able to form any reliable estimate of the expenditure requisite to cultivate an acre, and they have been deceived by the statement that the estate produced a certain number of hundredweights without ascertaining correctly of how many acres these were the produce, and thus, although 600 cwts. from 100 acres would yield a handsome profit, the same quantity from 200 acres would not more than pay the cultivation expenses; from this cause it will be obvious that nothing can be more fallacious than the system of valuation by the number of acres. As a general rule an estate yielding less than 5 cwts. an acre, is not worth more than £20 an acre, whilst an estate giving 10 cwts. is certainly worth £60, and so on in an increasing ratio. The net value of a cwt. of coffee on the trees is about 50s. both in India and Ceylon, and it will cost fully the value of 3 cwts. for the ordinary annual cultivation expenses per acre, exclusive of the crop expenses. An estate of 200 acres, yielding 5 cwts. per acre only, would not give therefore an annual profit of more than £1,000, whilst the same extent, if giving 10 cwts. per acre, would clear £3,500.

In the valuation of estates also, care should be had to take a fair average of three or four years, nothing being more common than for the value to be fixed on the basis of a bumper crop, the result of extraordinary manuring and pruning. As a rule, a very safe mode of valuation will be found to allow £10 for every hundredweight per acre that the estates actually produce above the amount required for upkeep, which is already stated to be about 3 cwts. Thus, an estate giving 6 cwts. per acre will be valued at £30 per acre, and one giving 10 cwts. would be £70. With young estates not yet in bearing, there cannot be a better mode of valuing than to allow a liberal interest for the risk and toil on the sum that the work done should actually have cost, always supposing that such work has been efficiently performed. There are of course exceptional cases, where from immediate neighbourhood to railways, large towns, etc., extraordinary prices may be given, but these are out of the operation of the general rules which should guide the planter in his investments.

CHAPTER XII.

ALTHOUGH the ripe coffee fruit is eagerly devoured by birds, monkeys, jackals, squirrels, and numerous other vermin, the tree itself has few enemies, and is subject to fewer diseases than most plants which are like it, of exotic growth, and cultivated largely by mankind for the sake of their produce.

The disease known as rot has been already referred to, and is simply the result of excessive moisture and imperfect ventilation, and deficient evaporation. The obvious remedy will be to assist the drainage of the soil and to keep the trees so thin by pruning that the air can freely circulate, and every glimpse of sunshine penetrate through the trees. In newly planted land, trees will frequently be noticed which, after a fort-night's dry weather succoeding the rainy season, begin to droop and turn yellow, and finally die off, apparently without any cause; but if these plants are carefully examined, they will be found to have lost all their bark at the level of the ground, and to be completely ringed. This is neither more nor less than the result of being planted too deep—the bark has rotted and been rubbed off by the chafing of the tree; occasionally, also, trees will be found which have worn a hole round their stems with continual agitation in the wind and rain, and this forms a funnel to catch and keep all the rain that trickles down the stem, and thereby rots the root. Both these defects are, however, within the control of the planter; but of the evils beyond his power the worst are undoubtedly the Borer and the Bug.

The former of these is a white or brownish grub, being the larva of one of the numerous small flying beetles common in the tropics. These breed in rotten and decaying timber, and find, therefore, every encouragement in coffee estates. These beetles eat a small hole, resembling the puncture of a gimlet, horizontally into the tree; they then undergo the transformation . into the grub, and continue their devastations perpendicularly both up and down the tree, until the tree dies. The part of the tree above their entrance generally gives unmistakable indications at once of their presence, and if these are noticed, and the tree cut off at the place where the perforation is seen, the grub will be found inside, and the lower portion of the tree will be saved and ultimately send out a sucker to supply the place of the lost stem. But it frequently occurs that large trees with heavy crops on them fall victims to this pest, and then it becomes necessary to root up the old tree and plant a fresh seedling in its place. The beetles may be observed flying about in numbers in the evenings after rain in March, April, and May, and if bright fires of weeds, grass, etc., are lighted on the various roads and other vacant places in the estates, they will be attracted by the blaze and light, and fly into the fires. This method has been found very efficacious, and is neither expensive or difficult of execution. It may be remarked that the borer is most abundant in rather dry localities, and is not so trouble-some in virgin forest land as in what has been already described as bamboo land.

Far more destructive, however, than the borer is the coffee-bug, a full description of which will be found in the succeeding chapter, which embodies the report made by Dr. Gardner to the Ceylon Government on the subject, and which is given at length in the very able work on the island lately published by Sir Emerson Tennent. It is somewhat remarkable that although the bug has appeared in all the coffee growing districts of India, it has never proved really destructive except in the district of Coorg, where it has almost caused the abandoning of some estates; but in Wynaad, the Neilgherries, and Mysore, it has never given cause for anxiety, as its appearance has been only partial, and it does not spread and engross the estates in the manner it has been found to do in Ceylon.

CHAPTER XIII.

NOTE.

THE COFFEE BUG.—(*Lecanium Coffee.*—Walker.)

THE following notice of the Coccus, known in Ceylon as the "Coffee Bug," and of the singularly destructive effects produced by it on the plants, has been prepared chiefly from a memoir presented to the Ceylon Government by the late Dr. Gardner, in which he traces the history of the insect from its first appearance in the coffee districts until it had established itself more or less permanently in all the estates in full cultivation throughout the island.

The first thing that attracts attention on looking at a coffee-tree which has for some time been infested by this coccus, is the number of brownish, wart-like bodies that stud the young shoots, and occasionally the margins on the underside of the leaves. Each of these warts, or scales, is a transformed female, containing a large number of eggs, which are hatched within it.

When the young ones come out from their nest they run about over the plant, looking very much like diminutive wood-lice, and at this period there is no apparent distinction between male and female. Shortly after being hatched, the males seek the underside of the leaves, whilst the females prefer the young shoots as a place of abode. If the undersurface of a leaf be examined, it will be found to be studded, particularly on its basal half, with minute yellowish-white specks of an oblong form. These are the larvæ of the males undergoing transformation into pupæ beneath their own skins. Some of those specks are always in a more advanced state than the others, the full grown ones being whitish and scarcely a line long. Some of this size are translucent, the insect having escaped, the darker ones have it still within, of an oblong form, with the rudiment of a wing on each side attached to the lower part of the thorax, and closely applied to the sides. The legs are six in number, the four hind ones being directed backwards, the anterior forwards (a peculiarity not occurring in other insects), the two antennæ are also inclined backwards, and from the tail. protrude three short bristles, the middle one thinner and longer than the rest.

When the transformation is complete, the mature insect makes its way from beneath the pellucid case.* All its organs having then attained their full size, the head is subglobular, with two rather prominent black eyes, and two antennæ, each with eleven joints, hairy throughout, and a tuft of rather longer hairs at the apices; the legs are also hairy, the wings are horizontal, of an obovate oblong shape, membranous, and extending a little further than the bristles of the tail. They have only two nerves, neither of which reaches so far as the lips; one of them runs close to the costal margin, and is much thicker than the other,.

* Mr. Westwood, who observed the operation in one species, states 'hat they escape backwards, the wings being extended flatly over the head.

which branches off from its base, and skirts along the inner margin; behind the wings is attached a pair of minute halteres of peculiar form. The possession of wings would appear to be the cause why the full-grown male is more rarely seen on the coffee bushes than the female.

The female, like the male, attaches herself to the surface of the plant, the place selected being usually the young shoots; but she is also to be met with on the margins of the undersides of the leaves (on the upper surface neither the male nor the female ever attach themselves), but unlike the male, which derives no nourishment from the juices of the tree (the mouth being obsolete in the perfect state), she punctures the cuticle with a proboscis (a very short three-jointed promuscis) springing, as it were, from the breast, but capable of being greatly porrected, and inserted in the cuticle of the plant, and through this she abstracts her nutriment. In the early pupa state the female is easily distinguishable from the male by being more elliptical and much more convex. As she increases in size the skin distends and she becomes more smooth and dry, the rings of the body become effaced, and losing entirely the form of an insect, she presents for some time a yellowish pustular shape, but ultimately assumes a roundish conical form, of a dark-brown colour.*

* There are many other species of the Coccus tribe in Ceylon, some (Pseudococcus) never appearing as a scale, the female wrapping herself up in a white cottony exudation. Many species nearly allied to the true Coccus infest common plants about gardens, such as the Nerium Oleander, Plumeria, Acuminata, and others with milky juices. Another subgenus (Ceroplastes), the female of which produces a protecting waxy material, infests the Gendurassa Vulgaris, the Fureraea Gigantea, the Jak Tree, Mango, and other common trees.

Until she has nearly reached her full size she still possesses the power of locomotion, and her six legs are easily distinguishable in the under surface of her corpulent body; but at no period of her existence has she wings. It is about the period of her obtaining full size that impregnation takes place (Reaumur has described the singular manner in which this occurs—*Mém.*, tom iv.), after which the scale becomes somewhat more conical, assumes a darker colour, and at length is permanently fixed to the surface of the plant, by means of a cottony substance interposed between it and the vegetable cuticle to which it adheres. The scale, when full grown, exactly resembles in miniature the hat of a Cornish miner, there being a narrow rim at the base, which gives increased surface of attachment. It is about one-eighth of an inch in diameter by about one-twelfth deep, and it appears perfectly smooth to the naked eye, but it is in reality studded all over with a multitude of very minute warts, giving it a dotted appearance; it is entirely destitute of hairs except the margin, which is ciliated. The number of eggs contained in one of the scales is enormous, amounting in a single one to six hundred and ninety-one. The eggs are of an oblong shape, of a pale fresh colour, and perfectly smooth. A few small yellowish maggots are sometimes found with the eggs, these are the larvæ* of insects, the eggs of which have been deposited in the female while the scale was soft. They

---

* Of the parasitic Chalcidiæ, many genera of which are well known to deposit their eggs in the soft coccus, viz., Encystus, Coccophagus, Pteromalus, Mesoscla, Agonioneurus, besides Apidius, a minutely-sized genus of Ichneumonidæ. Most, if not all these genera are Singhalese.

escape when mature by cutting a small round hole in the dorsum of the scale.

It is not till after this pest has been on an estate for two or three years that it shows itself to an alarming extent. During the first year a few only of the ripe scales are seen scattered over the bushes, generally on the younger shoots; but that year's crop does not suffer much, and the appearance of the tree is little altered. The second year, however, brings a change for the worse. If the young shoots and the underside of the leaves be now examined, the scales will be found to have become much more numerous, and with them appears a multitude of white specks, which are the young scales in a much less forward state. The clusters of berries now assume a black sooty look, and a great number of them fall off before coming to maturity; the general health of the tree also begins to fail, and it acquires a blighted appearance. A loss of crop is this year sustained, but to no great extent. The third year brings about a more serious change; the whole plant acquires a black hue, appearing as if soot had been thrown over it in great quantities. This is caused by the growth of a parasitic fungus* over the shoots and the upper surface of the leaves, forming a fibrous coating, somewhat resembling velvet or felt. This never makes its appearance till the insect has been a long time on the bush, and it probably owes its existence there to an unhealthy condition of the juices of

* Racodium, species of this genus are not confined to the coffee plant alone in Ceylon, but follow the " bugs " in their attacks on other bushes. It appears like a dense interlaced mesh of fibres, each made up of a single series of minute oblong vesicles applied end to end.

the leaf, consequent on the irritation produced by the coccus, since it never visits the upper surface of the leaf until it has fully established itself on the lower. At this period the young shoots have an exceedingly disgusting look from the dense mass of yellow pustular bodies forming on them, the leaves get shrivelled, and the tree becomes conspicuous in the row; the black ants are assiduous in their visits to them; two-thirds of the crop is lost, and on many trees not a single berry forms.

As far as it is possible to ascertain, the coffee bushes were not affected before 1843, when Captain Robertson first observed the pest on his estate, Lapalla Galla, whence it spread eastward through other estates, and finally reached all the other estates in the island. It or a very closely allied species has been observed in the botanic garden at Peradonia, on the citrus acida, psidium pomiferum, myrtas zeylanica, rosa indica, cureya arborea, vitex negundo, and other plants. The coffee coccus has generally been first observed in moist hollow places, sheltered from the wind, and thence it has spread itself even over the driest and most exposed parts of the islands, and in some estates after attaining a maximum, it has gradually declined, but has shown a liability to reappear, especially in low sheltered situations, and it is believed to prevail most extensively in wet seasons. It is easily transmitted from one estate to another, while in its earlier stages, on the clothes of human beings, and in various other ways which will readily suggest themselves. Dr. Gardner, after careful consideration and minute examination of estates, arrived at the conclusion that all remedies suggested up to that time had utterly failed, and that none at once cheap and effectual was likely to be discovered. He seems also to have been of opinion that the insect was not under human control; and that even if it should disappear, it would only be when it had worn itself out as other blights have been known to do in some mysterious way. Whether this may prove to be the case or not, is still very uncertain, but everything observed by Dr. Gardner tended to indicate the permanency of the pest.

CHAPTER XIV.

NOTWITHSTANDING what has already been said, some of the readers of this may be glad of further assistance in forming their judgment on the merits and demerits of the pursuit known as Coffee Planting, and for their benefit the following extracts are appended. A writer in his " Impressions of the West Indies," says :—

" Anything in the way of cultivation more beautiful or more fragrant than a coffee plantation I had not conceived, and oft did I say to myself that if ever I became, from health or otherwise, a cultivator of the soil within the tropics, I would cultivate the coffee plant, even although I did so irrespective altogether of the profits that might be derived from so doing. Much has been written, and not without justice, of the rich fragrance of an orange grove, and at home we ofttimes hear of the sweet odours of a bean field. I have, too, often enjoyed in the Carse of Stirling, and elsewhere in Scotland, the balmy breezes as they swept over the latter, particularly when the sun had burst out with unusual strength after a shower of rain. I have likewise in Martinique, Santa Cruz, Jamaica, and Cuba inhaled the breezes wafted from the orangeries, — but not for a moment would I compare either with the exquisite aromatic odours from a coffee plantation in full bloom, when the hill-side—covered over with regular rows of the shrubs, with their millions of their jasmine-like flowers—showers down upon you as you ride up between the plants, a perfume of the most delicately delicious description. 'Tis worth going to the West Indies to see the sight and inhale the perfume."

From the "Colombo Observer" of this date we extract the following :—

" The Gona Adika Coffee Estate, property of the late Mr. Tucker, was sold for £30,000, the total extent being nearly 1,000 acres, more than 800 of which were in coffee. The property was bought on account of the mortgage, and it is understood that the purchase price was £9,000 less than the encumbrances on the estate. This is but a type of numerous cases. Prices have been good for years back, but numbers of coffee proprietors got hopelessly involved in the bad times, and latterly, increased expenditure here seems to have kept pace with the rise in prices. Still some persons must profit, or the pursuit would not be persevered in. But the actual working planters who have made fortunes, or even secured a competency, might be counted with but a slight mental effort."

Of still more value is the testimony of Sir Emerson Tennent, as he had the most ample opportunities of making himself acquainted with all opinions and details in the matter, and he writes as follows :—

" Whatever may be the ascertained advantages of Ceylon in point of soil, temperature and moisture, and however bountiful may be the yield of the plants, the speculation must always be estimated in connection with the cost and vicissitudes with which it is unhappily associated. Anxiety must be inseparable from an undertaking exclusively dependent on immigrant labour, and liable to be affected at the most critical moment by its capricious fluctuations. No temptation of wages, and no prospect of advantage, has hitherto availed to overcome the repugnance of the Singhalese and Kandyans to engage in any work on estates, except the first process of felling the forests. Every subsequent operation must be carried on by Coolies from Malabar and the Coromandel coast, whose arrival is uncertain and whose departure being influenced by causes arising in India, may be precipitated by the most unforeseen occurrences.* These labourers have to be remunerated at high rates in the silver currency of India, the value of which fluctuates with the exchanges, and fed on rice imported for their exclusive consumption, burdened with all the charges of freight, duty, and carriage to the hills. The crop, when saved on the estate, has either to encounter the risks incident to transport by hand, through mountains as yet unopened by roads, or the chances of deterioration to which it is exposed in bullock carts during long journeys to the coast.

" Where circumstances enable the proprietor to be resident on his own estate, and to superintend its operations and control its expenditure in person, few colonial pursuits present attractions superior to those exhibited by Ceylon, either as to actual enjoyment or

---

* In 1858 the number of Tamil labourers arriving in Ceylon was 96,000. The number taking their departure from the island was 50,000.

reasonable returns for investment. But where the capitalist is helplessly reliant on the honour and services of a representative on his distant possessions, under circumstances in which few have the resolution to resist stimulants and the usual devices for diversifying monotony and overcoming the *ennui* attendant on isolation and solitude, property of this kind is accompanied by inextricable risks and anxieties, and the owner will be often tempted to ascribe to bad faith or neglect, the disappointments, outlay, and losses which are in reality attributable to ordinary vicissitudes rather than to the infidelity of agents."

The attention of the reader is particularly called to the last paragraph, and where the investment contemplated is in conjunction with a Joint Stock Company the utmost care should also be taken to ascertain the qualifications of the directors and managers for their self-imposed duties, as instances are not uncommon of fully three-fourths of the number of the directors of a company being entirely ignorant of everything regarding coffee, except perhaps, of how it is drunk, and as a matter of course, those who do really understand the management are frequently in a minority on many important questions ; further, let not the incautious speculator be tempted by what is called "a guarantee of a minimum dividend," for a grosser delusion was never practised on the British public. In most cases it means simply that the vendor of the property or directors of the company are to receive so much more than the real value of it, that if they get that amount they can afford to pay the interest out of it ; and, if on the other hand, the guaranteed dividend has really to be earned out of the profits, the guarantor will naturally do his best to keep the expenditure as low as possible, and thus most probably to starve the property, on the principle of *après moi le deluge*, little caring that the unlucky shareholder finds himself at the expiration of the term of guarantee in possession of a neglected and exhausted estate. If the project is really *bona fide*, it will yield 15 to 20 per cent. without a guarantee, which will always tend to a parsimonious and injurious policy. If on the other hand, the affair is what is styled in city phraseology "a swindle," the return of a portion of "the plunder" in the shape of "guaranteed dividend," will be a very small consolation to the shareholder. At least nine-tenths of the subscribers to the various Tea and Coffee Companies have no means of satisfying themselves as to the character of the speculation, except from such documents as may be produced by the directors and their friends or the representations of the financial associations through means of which these undertakings are commonly introduced, and whatever, therefore, be the source of information, it is seldom wholly impartial or disinterested. Of all projects, the inexperienced speculator should be careful in dealing with those introduced by financial associations. In the first place a very considerable sum has to be paid as commission, which in one way or other comes out of the shareholders' pocket, and in the second, as the responsibility of the introducers ends with the allotment of shares, the interest of the shareholders is not cared for and they will frequently find themselves exposed to vexatious litigation, or pledged to arrangements most injurious to all except the directors and other officers whom tho introducers have selected.

From what has been already said it will have been gathered that the speculation, or enterprise as it should more fitly be termed, of coffee planting, is a very legitimate subject for the formation of joint-stock companies. There are, it will have been seen, considerable advantages to be gained by prosecuting the project on an extended scale. The European management both in England and abroad forming no inconsiderable part of the expense, it will always be found advantageous to afford full employment to this description of labour; and an able, active manager can superintend 1500 or 2000 acres with very little more trouble than half that extent would entail. Again, the expenses in England of a well-constituted company need be little more than the amount saved by their acting as their own agents in the sale of their produce. A vast proportion of the failures amongst the planting community have resulted from insufficient capital, and the enormous interest which the borrower has been obliged to pay for funds sufficient to bring his concern to a successful issue; but, with a joint-stock company neither of these exigencies are likely to occur, and in the present state of the market the only cause which should affect the prospects of the undertaking is the very material question of management; but where this is really efficient with a due regard to economy, few enterprises present a more certain prospect of liberal returns than coffee planting.

APPENDIX.

_____ *Estate*

Daily Report _____ 186

WORKS, Etc.	E. Superintdts.	N. Superintdts.	1st.	2nd.	3rd.	4th.	Total.
Nurseries							
Planting { Clearing							
Planting { Pitting							
Planting { Planting							
Weeding							
Pruning							
Building							
Trenching							
Roads							
Manuring							
Cattle							
Tappal Cooly							
Crop. { Preparing for Crop							
Crop. { Picking							
Crop. { Pulping, etc.							
Total							

Weather _____

_____ *Superintendent*

Form No. 1.

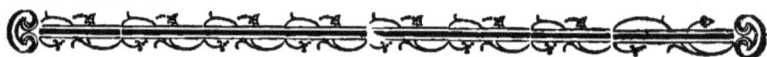

_____ *Estate*

Daily Report, ___ 18 ___

_____ *Estate*

*Daily Report*_____ 186

WORKS, Etc.								
	E. Superintdts.	N. Superintdts.	1st.	2nd.	3rd.	4th.	Total.
Nurseries							
Weeding..							
Pruning...							
Building...							
Trenching							
Roads							
Manuring							
Cattle							
Tappal Cooly................................							
Crop. { Preparing for Crop..........................							
Picking							
Pulping, etc.							
Total.....................							

Weather _____

_____ *Superintendent*

Form No. 2.

_____ *Estate*

Daily Report, ___ 18 _____

_____*Estate*

*Daily Report*_____ 186

WORKS, Etc.	E. Superintdts.	N. Superintdts.	1st.	2nd.	3rd.	4th.	Total.
Nurseries...........................							
Planting. { Clearing...........................							
Pitting..............................							
Planting...........................							
Weeding.............................							
Pruning..............................							
Building.............................							
Trenching..........................							
Roads...............................							
Manuring							
Cattle...............................							
Tappal Cooly......................							
Total...............							

Weather _____

_____*Superintendent*

Form No. 3.

_____*Estate*

*Daily Report,*___ 18____

Tools			Total Rupees.
Stock			
Transport			
Miscellaneous ...			
Superintendence .			
Total Rupees...			

Tool Return.	Cattle Return.				
		Cows.	Bullocks.	Calves.	Buffaloes.
Momaties					
Pickaxes					
Hoes	Last Account.				
Axes	Sold............				
Billhooks	Bought				
Crowbars	Died				
Pruning Knives	Increase				
Grass Knives...					
Adzes............					
Sledgehammers					
Saws	Total...				

Date.	WEATHER.	Nurseries.	Clearing.	Pitting.	Planting.	Weeding.	Pruning.	Manuring.	Building.							Transport.	Miscellaneous.	Daily Totals.
1																		
2																		
3																		
4																		
5																		
6																		
7																		
8																		
9																		
10																		
11																		
12																		
13																		
14																		
15																		
16																		
17																		
18																		
19																		
20																		
21																		
22																		
23																		
24																		
25																		
26																		
27																		
28																		
29																		
30																		
31																		
	Totals																	

Dr.   Superintendent in Account with   Estate   Cr.

GENERAL REMARKS.

Clearing _____

Pitting _____

Planting _____

Weeding _____

Buildings _____

Roads _____

Crop _____

Miscellaneous _____

HARRILD, PRINTER, LONDON.

www.ingramcontent.com/pod-product-compliance
Lightning Source LLC
Chambersburg PA
CBHW031453270326
41930CB00007B/977